REFLECTIONS
TO MY SISTERS

BY
MONALISA SMITH

MOTHERS
FOR JUSTICE & EQUALITY

Reflections to My Sisters

REFLECTIONS
TO MY SISTERS

MOTHERS
FOR JUSTICE & EQUALITY

FIRST PRINTING

*"We envision a world where it is
not normal or acceptable for children
to be murdered or incarcerated."*

©2014
Mothers for Justice and Equality

TABLE OF CONTENTS

Introduction: A Letter to My Sisters

Reflections:

Acknowledgments

About Mothers for Justice and Equality

About the Author

Reflections to My Sisters

Dear Sisters,

I want to share some personal reflections with you that have often kept me awake in the early morning hours writing about our journey as mothers, daughters and women of color living in a world in which some of us are silenced by fear and left to feel invisible.

I felt the urgency to share the reflections with you as if you were waiting for an answer to something pressing on your heart.

My heart is filled with so much joy and I want to share that joy with you. I wrote this book of reflections in hope that the special gift inside of you will be released as my gift was released; Fear, anxiety and confusion were my constant companions but I overcame my fears and stepped out on faith, never to look back on what I left behind.

My prayer is that each reflection will touch your heart and encourage you to begin your personal journey of finding that special gift that is inside of you.

I have seen so many women find their gift. These women have been through some of the most difficult moments in life and discovered that their circumstances did not keep them in bondage; it was their secret (s) that was hindering them from finding their gift.

Reflections to My Sisters

I saw these secret (s) bringing release and the gifts start to come forth. Interestingly, when they released their secret (s) it opened the door for others to be freed. These women are my heroes; they are my sisters who have touched my heart and soul in so many ways that I hope to share with you in this book of reflections.

I dedicate this book of reflections to a circle of strong sisters in the struggle. Together we will be the Change Makers.

In peace,

Monalisa Smith
Founder and President
Mothers for Justice and Equality

Reflections to My Sisters

Reflections to My Sisters

The keeper of the secret

Who is the keeper of the secret? She is the one who holds the key to set her sisters free. She is the daughter that had the biggest dream, the most beautiful smile and the biggest heart. She is the daughter that was hurt and told not to speak those lies in public. She is the daughter that was passed around, shared and told "it's your fault" by the ones she loved and trusted the most. The young woman who found comfort in the alcohol, drugs and sex that she used to numb the pain that was felt in her soul from the hurt and abuse she suffered as a child. Who is the keeper of the secret that holds the key to our freedom? As a child, she was trained by shame, guilt and pain to keep the secret. Mothers, aunts, sisters and grandmothers unknowingly were the best trainers; they too were taught to keep the secret. Today, I am sending her a letter in hope that she will use her key to set her sisters free from physical and emotional abuse, homelessness, substance abuse, loss of a loved one, and so much more.

Dear Sister,

Are you the keeper of the secret? If so you need to know that there is a key that was planted in you when you entered your mother's womb; Every unwanted touch, every hurtful word, alcohol, drugs, sex and other things which you know of buried that key deep inside you.

Release the secret and find the key that will lead you to your destiny. In doing so, you will save yourself and others that have lost their way. You must find a safe space where you can trust that there will be no judgment and other people will accept you right where you are because you hold a special gift inside of you that needs to be found and released.

I believe before you were conceived in your mother's womb a seed, a vision was planted in you. It's still there and your job is to find it. Please know that it's not your past that is holding you back, it is your secret. Do you remember the little girl, before it started? She is still there. It's the secret that you have been taught to keep that holds the key to you moving into your destiny. Don't be afraid to dream. You hold the key to your freedom.

Reflections to My Sisters

Reflections to My Sisters

Who am I?

I am a mother and a daughter forced to adapt to a system that was designed to teach me who I am.

I am a survivor taught by those that came before me how to survive and not to conform to the sting of injustice that could steal my identity and put my children at-risk.

I am a black woman, a mother, a daughter, living in a world that sees my color and gender but not my gifts or talents. At times, I am invisible.

I am a mother raising brown and black children in neighborhoods where murder and incarceration of children is normal and children are not allowed to experience normal adolescent behaviors that would shape their identity and nurture their creativity.

I am a mother who must tell her son at an early age that because of who he is, he will be pre-judged for no reason at all but he must maintain complete emotional control at all times – to protect his life from being stolen from him.

I find myself being silent in the face of injustice in order to survive. I find myself being invisible in order to maintain my identity and protect my children.

As I am sitting in a unity circle with my sisters who look like me, who share my struggle; I know that I am not alone. This gives me hope in knowing that together we can create change for our sons and daughters, the next generation of leaders who will not be silent in the face of injustice.

Our youth hold the key to our future.

Reflections to My Sisters

Here I am

I am a keeper of a secret. I hold a key to set my sisters free. I am the one that had the biggest smile, the trusting heart and the belief that life would treat me fairly. Until one day when my sister and I were given to strangers who were to love, nurture and teach us to respect our minds, body and soul; it was a system created to define us; a system that thought it knew what was best for my mother, sister and me.

We had the unwanted touch, the unwanted words and we were made to believe that this was how love and nurture was supposed to feel. As our body developed, so did our sexual and emotional abuse, it kept perfect pace.

One rainy day my sister disappeared, leaving me to hold two secrets. I looked around for her, I inquired about her and I asked where did she go? Only to find silence; at a very young age I became the keeper of her secret and mine, a little girl alone with two secrets.

Here I am a woman at a very early age. I was screaming but no one could hear me or see me. My abuser saw my body but not my soul.

Here I am silenced by a system that was supposed to protect my sister and me. I was taken from my mother and promised a better future only to find emotional and sexual abuse as a child.

Here I am aged out of my sexual and emotional abuse, only to find physical abuse at the hands of a man who vowed to love me for better or worst - he was my husband. He was supposed to love me and protect our children, and his love hurt me. Fear and loneliness became my constant companions, I escaped from my physical abuse with two beautiful children.

Here I am a mother who vows to protect her children from a system that failed me; a system that promised to protect me and help me to grow into a strong black woman.

Reflections to My Sisters

I kept silent and I stayed invisible in hope that my children would not endure my past, but will have the opportunity to live in my future. I am learning in my sister circle that my future is greater than my past. I am so grateful for my sisters in the circle that held the key to unlock my secret.

My sister did not fully know me but she loved me so much that she overcame her fear to reveal to me that she was the keeper of a secret that held the key to set me free. I felt like I had found my sister that was lost in my childhood, and I was no longer carrying her secret and mine.

Reflections to My Sisters

Mother's, keepers of Humanity

In her perfect love she is a keeper of humanity. Mothers were created with a special gift, a womb designed to nurture a seed and give birth to a new hope. All women are born with a special gift. Some choose to be mothers and give birth to children, others choose to be leaders and give birth to great ideas that change the world for the better. It is the gift that we share that bonds us together as keeper of humanity.

A mother had a special seed planted in her womb that the enemy of humanity wanted to destroy. In her perfect love she fled to shield and protects the seed from being destroyed. The enemy knew that she was carrying a seed of hope that would allow all of humanity to reconcile with its creator, so the enemy set out to find and destroy the mother and her seed. However, he did not anticipate the strong love between the mother and her seed - it was beyond his comprehension.

The love between the mother and the seed was so strong that the mother was willing to giving up her life to ensure its safety. The mother fled from the enemy. She left all she knew and hid from his reach. She sought the help of strangers to protect the seed from being found and destroyed. The enemy of humanity became angry and began to cause confusion with daughters and sons who were to be mothers and fathers. Innocent lives were stolen and confusion was prevalent in the land. The womb of mothers began to cry out for mercy and balance in the universe was no more - leaving humanity with an urgency need to end the violence and captivity that was taking the lives of its children.

The enemy in all of his infinite wisdom and deception could not create a womb to birth a seed into the world. So the woman who had this precious gift became his greatest adversary. The woman vowed to protect her seed by bruising his head at every chance she got. The enemy knew when a daughter was to be born into the world that there was likelihood that she will be a keeper of humanity.

Reflections to My Sisters

Although it would not be an easy task for the daughter to accomplish - in perfect love she would give birth to hope through a very painful and agonizing process. At times the pain would be too much for her to bear but she will continue to push and bear down knowing that hope is at hand. The moment she gives birth, the joy of motherhood will cause her to forget the pain. At that moment a new hope is born into the world, a hope that will to restore the balance in the universe.

Our sons and daughters will finally be freed from bondage.

Reflections to My Sisters

A voice of hope in a time of uncertainty

Has my son or daughter life become another statistic lost to street violence, remembered by marches and rallies, embraced by emotions of fear, anger, and frustration of strangers?

Has my son or daughter's life become a distant memory replaced by another mother's loss, remembered only in my silence, fears and tears?
Has my son's or daughter's life become known as another loved one lost to senseless street violence by friends, community members, civic leaders and relatives who hopelessly watch not knowing what to say or feel for me or my children?

As my numbness gives way and the sweet energy of my son or daughter enters, I can feel my three companions, loneliness, anxiety and fear – leave, and hope begins to move in. At that moment, I remember my son or daughter's life being more than a distant memory, a forgotten march or rally, but instead, it is a call to humanity for justice and equality to stand up for hope for all of God's children.
For in this hope we are all saved.

Reflections to My Sisters

Reflections to My Sisters

The face of injustice

I often wonder what injustice looks like. Does it have a face, a personality, and a voice? Or is it just a spirit that seeks out someone who is weary, tried, fearful, or blinded by ignorance to carry out its wicked deeds?

All women who seek justice for themselves and their children can't help but wonder what injustice looks like. As daughters, we were always taught to believe that it was the face of racism, but when we look around us, all races of women seem to be experiencing some type of injustice.

Injustice seems to overpower our emotional state of mind, causing us to be physically ill at times, and lack motivation to be successful. It takes a greater toll on those of us with the least means with which to fight back. We see higher levels of cancerous diseases; premature births and physical ailments in our sisters living in impoverished conditions.

Injustice uses those who are fearful of change and blinded by ignorance to block opportunity. It establishes barriers that kept us divided. It takes away the future for generations of daughters who are coming behind us.

All women, from the moment we enter into the world met injustice. Our hope is in those women who came before us. They fought a good fight for justice and equality and left us a road map to end injustice. They were our mothers, grandmothers and aunts. Some grew old and others grew tried.

Sadly, there was no one to pick up the mantel and stand for justice and equality. So the injustice grew stronger and wiser. Eventually, taking over our neighborhoods, taking root in our homes and community. We begin to see our children exhibit signs of self-hate by committing violent acts against one other. It was called "black on black crime" but it was our children, losing their sense of identity and falling victims to injustice.

What does injustice look like? I wonder does it look like me.

Reflections to My Sisters

Reflections to My Sisters

Listen

As I sit quietly and watch with hope, I can't help but wonder does anyone hear what I hear. Does anyone hear the sound of the trumpet, the voices of hope? Does anyone see the mothers marching?

I can't help but wonder in all the noise and voices of opinions and reasoning does anyone hear a loud trumpet that is followed by small voices, followed by mothers marching for peace.

I hear the mothers saying listen to the sound of my heart that is beating for justice and equality. Listen to the sound of the trumpet that is blowing for victory and listen to the sound of our feet marching, breaking the wall that separates us from the promise of peace, justice and equality.

Listen to the voices, transforming my sisters into leaders. Listen to the voices of the hopeless sounding hopeful, and the voice of the weak gaining strength.

I can hear the voices of change rising above the voice of reasoning and opinions, it sounds like freedom, it sounds like hope.

Listen with your heart.

Reflections to My Sisters

Reflections to My Sisters

Some days. Other days.

Some days I feel the world belongs to me and the sky is the limit. I find myself singing songs of hope and victory; I find myself glowing in front of strangers. I find myself believing that I am beautiful and loved by someone special. I am unstoppable.

In my mind I feel the warmth of the sun shining on my face; I find myself sitting peaceful near a beautiful oak tree, in front of a reflection lake. The sound of the soft winds blowing sounds like whispers in my ear. I hear poems of love and peace being spoken to me. The soft winds feel like a soft touch that caress against my body. I am in total peace as if I am floating above the clouds and no one can see me or feel me. It's just the universe and me with no such thing as time; its endless, there is no beginning and there is no end to the love, peace and tranquility I am feeling. It's my creator and me together at last.

Suddenly, I am awakening to a loud noise, it sounds like sirens moving toward me, it sound like every other day; a place where I live and work; a place with loud noise, anxiety and fear. The noise of the sirens stops, it's followed by a voice of pain and fear crying out for mercy. The soft winds I felt on my face that caressed my body have turned into strong stormy winds that are whipping against my skin. My glow is no more, it has been replaced with complete horror. My heart is broken again and I am yearning for my some day to return and my other day to go away forever, they are becoming to much for me to bear.

My heart, body and soul desire more some days and less other days.

Reflections to My Sisters

Reflections to My Sisters

Mom, I'm free.

Today I joined a sister circle and got freed. I'm no longer angry with you. I understand how difficult life was for you. I know that you were giving me what you knew. You would be proud to know that I am free.

Mom, it was a seed that was inside me that kept me in so much pain. Every time I tried to tell you about the abuse you pushed me away. I felt so alone and dirty. I didn't feel like I was anyone's little girl. I could not feel myself anymore. My hurt became my normal. At first I tried to hold on to the first time we met - when I was born. I felt so much love; I knew I was your bundle of joy.

Mom, as I grew older things suddenly started to change. I didn't feel like I was your bundle of joy anymore. I felt your loneliness and your pain. I felt his touch. I felt blame and shame. Why did you let him hurt us? Why couldn't you get away? I remember seeing you and then not seeing you. I recall you being physically there but you were not the woman that held me in her arms and smiled at me. The soft touch, the sweet smell and the sound of laughter was gone. It was replaced with the scent of bitterness and shame.

Mom, why did you let him kill you? Why were you too afraid to run? I felt every blow, I heard every scream. You tried to fight back but he was too strong for you. You were my hero. You did not die in the struggle. You lived for me, but in your pain and shame you could not show me love because it hurt so bad.

Mom, you would be happy to know that I wasn't afraid to run. Mom, you would be happy to know that I am finally free. I got my liberty, mom. I am finally free. My daughters and sons, your grandchildren will no longer have to keep our secrets and be afraid to run.

Mom, you would be happy to know that our struggle was not in vein. So many daughters have read our story and they got freed too.

Reflections to My Sisters

Mom are you free? Does he still hold you in captivity? Have you forgiven him? Have you forgiven yourself, mom? I realize that you only did what you knew was normal. You fought the good fight and I am free. You are still my hero.

Mom, you can break the cycle of normal, love should not hurt. I would love to meet you again and feel the warm love I felt when we first met. See your smile and hear your laughter.

Mom, are you still there? If so, know that I love you and forgive you.

Forever yours, Your Daughter

Reflections to My Sisters

Reflections to My Sisters

Reflections to My Sisters

Would you wait?

Today I am starting a new life. I am leaving behind old habits and bad memories. My new life is going to take me on a journey that I will need to travel alone. On my journey I need to uncover a few things. I need to be completely honest and vulnerable with others and myself.

My old habits won't be comfortable on this journey. They will try to force me to quit but I won't be alone; I will have a few sisters with me. We will bond together and share our struggles.

Together, we will create a sister circle of trust. The circle will be completely closed so no one who is not invited can come in. We will begin to release our secrets and reflect on our journey. We will grow to understand that our past is not an indicator of future, but it can be used to fuel us forward.

Will you wait for me? I will need some time to get my life back. My past stole many of my prized processions; my children, my innocence, my self-esteem and so much more. I am going to have re-think some thing's and shed a few heavy personal things that have purposely held me back. I must admit that some of them I liked. I have to give up drugs, alcohol and meaningless sex; they won't be coming with me into my future. I will be searching for a treasure in side of me; it's my purpose, my vision, and my identity. I must go alone, with the support of my sisters, in order to overcome fear and stay focused so I don't miss it when it finally finds me.

I need you to understand that when I return, I will not be the same person anymore. My eyes, facial features and physical size might be the same. But my mind, body and soul will be transformed. You may see me but you may not know me.

Will you wait for me? If so, I will need you to forget my past and embrace my future. Are you willing to change for me; it will be vitally important that you leave all things behind that are memories of my past.

I need you to understand on my journey the old me will give away and a new me will emerge. The good things in my life will stay with me and the unpleasant things will be no more. I will begin the journey as a caterpillar and finish as a butterfly.

So will you wait for me?

Reflections to My Sisters

Reflections to My Sisters

Where are you Adam?

Dear Adam,

Raising our children alone in a world that does not value their gifts but has put in place a scheme to steal their identity and freedom is not easy. I am living in a village where losing sons and daughters to murder, incarceration and exploitation is an epidemic. My color and gender does not help -There are hidden obstacles put in place that block me from moving out of the desolate village. The barriers are designed to ensure that I am blinded from knowing my purpose and slowly lose a sense of self. It causes me to be silent and invisible on important matters that could save the lives of our children and restore hope to the village.

Adam, my nights and days are long and sometimes lonely as I wait for our son or daughter to return home from school or a normal social activity. There are constant reports of children lives being stolen from their mothers. So fear and anxiety has become a normal emotion for others and me.

Where are you Adam? It's been a while since the serpent stole our identity. I am sorry that I was weak and could not resist his temptation. I was lonely - you were always working in the garden. The serpent came to visit me daily, seducing me with his lies and his charm. He told me the forbidden fruit would make us closer and wiser. He told me you would spend more time with me. I thought I was doing something good for us.

Where are you Adam? I remember when our creator asked you what happened and you, in fear, blamed me. You did not protect me, but tried to save yourself.

Where are you Adam? My births are painful and the pain is tough to bear. The serpent is always waiting for an opportunity to kill our seed. He brings confusion and death to so many innocent children and incarcerates their parents, both physically and emotionally. But I vow to repay him for stealing our love and killing our children. By bruising his head every chance I get - this happens every time I give birth; bringing a new hope into the world.

Reflections to My Sisters

Where are you Adam? I remember hearing a story similar to ours. Your son had a beautiful wife and they traveled to a foreign land. The wife was so beautiful that the ruler of this land wanted to keep her. In fear for his life, he left his wife there. He did not protect her. Our creator in his faithful love rescued her and returned her to your son. You would be delighted to know your son became one of the most faithful friends of our creator; their friendship became the hope of mankind, it is his seed that brought prosperity to the land where you were the first-born.

Where are you Adam? So many of your sons have fallen; they seem to lose their way and like you, leave their wife to shoulder burden the blame alone.

Wives wombs mourn the loss of children and cry out to the creator for mercy.

Adam, the creator saw good in us again and sent his beautiful son who was birthed by one of my daughters into the earth. Yes, Adam another son was born into the earth. His love, faithfulness and commitment to fulfill his father's purpose saved us all and restored our relationship with the creator. His name is Jesus. Emanuel, which means God, is with us.

Where are you Adam? I know the creator has forgiven me and has sentenced the serpent to death for everything he has stolen from you and me. Through his son, Jesus Christ I am redeemed. Do you forgive me Adam? If so, turn back to your family.

We need you to protect us and restore the village.

I love and miss you Adam.

Forever yours,
Eve

Reflections to My Sisters

Reflections to My Sisters

Reflections to My Sisters

HOPE Speaks

Hope has a voice that speaks louder than words. Hope has a presence that is seen in mothers marching for peace.

Hope has the strength to take our past, present and future and create the perfect storm that can move us into a place of peace, love and harmony; a storm that could wash away our pain and frustration and restore a sense hope and unity back to our community.

In hopes perfect storm there will be strong winds that will blow away hate and shame. In hopes perfect storm there will be heavy rain that will wash away dirt and blame. The lightening would be so strong that it would strike anyone who gets in the way of the creation, the transformation of the community.

The perfect storm that hope brings, would restore hope to desolate land; after the storm, the sun will shin bright, a rainbow would appear and in this hope we will see the faces of change being re-born.

Reflections to My Sisters

Reflections to My Sisters

Do you trust me?

With your heart, body and soul. I am the one who promised to meet you where you are at and not to blame or judge you in your struggle. I am the one that will welcome you home, comfort and reassure you through it all.

Will you trust me with your heart, body and soul. I am the one that knew and kept you when you were weak and wanted to give up. I knew you before you were broken, we shared a special bond, and you were willing to trust me then with your heart, body and soul. Your innocence was sweet and your trust was pure. You trusted me with your heart, body and soul, you did not question our love or my faithfulness to you.

I am the one who rescued you when your life became too much to bear. It was me that touched you when you couldn't feel any more. You could not feel yourself, but I could feel you, I never stopped loving you. I never gave up on our hope, you felt hopeless and I felt hopeful. You felt abandoned and I felt closer than ever, in your loneliness, I drew closer to you.

When your smile faded, I was smiling at you, for us. When you fell I picked you up and carried you the rest of the way. My touch, my smile, and my scent was in the strangers you met along the way, they were my angels, sent to watch over you, while you found your way back to me. I never left you although you felt alone.

I need to know will you trust me with your body, mind and soul. I will meet you anywhere. We can leave together, but before we leave, I need to know will you trust me with your heart, body, and soul.

It is important to me that we are in agreement and you are truly committed to our relationship. You have the free will to surrender all to me, so will you trust me with it all.

I have always loved you with all my heart, body and soul. I gave it all up for you, so we could be together forever. Will you believe in me, love and trust me with your heart, body and soul? If so, I will wait for you.

Reflections to My Sisters

Reflections to My Sisters

Who's watching me?

Sometimes I feel like someone is watching me. I can't see them but I can feel their presence. At times its frightening and at times its welcomed.

I see hope and despair running parallel in my life, it's almost as if they are twins running in a race together. Maybe it's hope and despair watching me, as I am trying to find myself, my purpose in the world.

As I am running a race for hope and trying to out pace despair, I become afraid, so I cover my head so I won't be seen but I continue to feel the presence of someone watching me; it begins to cause me to be distracted and lose pace in the race.

I can't be afraid, I must be brave, I must believe that hope will protect me and I will out pace despair, because hope and me are running in the race together against despair.

So, I uncover my head so I can see better. I feel a sense of relief and I am running faster. I am no longer afraid. I realize that despair maybe watching me but hope is with me.

Hope is covering me in the race and it is I running parallel with despair. Although we are not twins we share similar characteristics, such as charisma, charm and stigma, both gaining momentum along the race.

I'm no longer afraid. I know it's both friend and foe; Its hope and despair running parallel for my soul both watching me run in the race for my liberty and freedom.

Reflections to My Sisters

Reflections to My Sisters

Finally, I can see

After living on the streets since the age of twelve, being honest, transparent and vulnerable in the presence of strangers was not going to be easy for me. I had to examine my past, which was painful, accept my present which I wasn't proud of, and see myself in a future which did not exist.

I had to let go of years of street survival training; skills I was taught at an early age of childhood - in lock up facilities, foster homes, living homeless, and taking jobs that I wasn't proud of to stay alive. My teachers had years of training, they were pimps, prostitutes and gang leaders, we all had one goal in common - survive the streets.

After years of street life the mere thought of letting down my shield was unheard of; It was all I had to protect me from a world that I felt hated me from the very beginning. I was ugly, fat, unwanted and always in somebody's way unless they wanted something from me.

I had to trust a circle of sisters who might not like the ugliness inside of me. They maybe disgusted with what I had to do to survive those streets. I knew letting my shield down would expose me and my secrets, but I wanted to survive. The life I was living did not feel right anymore. Something different inside of me was calling. I needed to make a choice, was I going to trust or walk away?

Today, I can finally see myself in my future. I have a vision and its look so much better than my past. I plan to visit my teachers who are still living on the streets and share some good news. I want them to know that life on the other side is not so bad after all, it's the secret (s) that keep us living on the streets. I hope they will be able to see themselves in their future.

I'm finally free. I am beautiful and appreciated. I have something to give back to the world.

Reflections to My Sisters

Reflections to My Sisters

What's beyond me?

How does the trees get air and perfectly lose their leaves and grow new leaves each season without anyone's help. How does a sea of purple, pink, yellow, green and a multitude of other colorful flowers grow as wild flowers in a field unkept by anyone; they seem to bloom perfectly in the right season every year; providing me with a picture perfect day.

How does the sun that has such power and capacity to destroy anything in its reach and beyond, shin so warmly and send just right amount heat to nurture my body, the trees, the flowers and the earth, without any instructions.

How does the moon stay behind the sun, until it's appropriate time to light up the earth, provide me, the birds and the trees with a dim light so we know it's time to sleep.

How does the birds fly so high in the sky without falling to the ground, knowing just when its time to fly to a different climate to stay warm.

How does the rainbow know when its time to shin so perfectly in the sky after a stormy day, reminding me that the storms of life will come to past and a rainbow of hope will always follow.

How does the universe stretch so wide, having no beginning and no end. Having complete influence over a large star in the sky "the sun" that has the power to eliminate creation as we know it in less than a moments notice, leaving behind not even a trace of creation.

There is so much beyond my imagination and comprehension, leaving me to know that I must be someone special for a perfect place to have been created just for me to learn, grow and be nurtured by a beautiful star and reminded daily of hope, in the sight of a rainbow, that faithfully appears after every storm in my life.

Reflections to My Sisters

Acknowledgments

This book of reflections was truly inspired by my relationship with the Holy Spirit. I would like to thank God for allowing me to share a positive message with so many of my Sisters. We share a strong bond that gives us the power to free each other from bondage and shame.
Planted inside of us is a special gift.

"When one releases the other was set free".

I would like to acknowledge the strong women who overcame fear and shame; they shared their secrets and set us all free. There are few words to describe the courage of my sister but I believe we are on our way in demonstrating our strength through faith and action.

Photos by Nancy Carbonado

ABOUT US

Who We Are

Mothers for Justice and Equality (MJE) harnesses and focuses the fierce love and protectiveness of mothers to create neighborhoods where playgrounds are safe and sidewalks are not threatening. MJE was founded in the fall of 2010 with the vision of a world in which it is never normal or acceptable for children to be murdered. Our children's lives have value and they must have the support of the entire community so that they are ensured a promising future.

Why Now?

For too long, neighborhood violence has left mothers fearful and without a voice. In one week during the summer of 2011, seven people were shot on four different Boston Streets. Six of the victims were men; one victim was a four-year-old boy playing in a park. In late September 2011, two boys on their way to buy a snack at the corner store were shot. One of the boys died, the other was seriously injured. One year earlier, Boston witnessed the killings of a two-year-old boy, his mother, and two men in their twenties in a single, horrific incident.

These stories are mirrored nationally, as well as in other Massachusetts cities. For too many people, this violence and loss of young lives has become unsurprising. We hear of violent incidents so often that we become desensitized to it, and this lack of sensitivity dehumanizes us all. It is time for that mind-set to change.

What We Believe

MJE believes that mothers are powerful change-makers in our communities. If given the right tools, mothers can become catalysts for change at home and advocates for change in their neighborhoods. Ultimately, MJE believes that change will occur as the internalized expectations of what is acceptable in our neighborhoods changes.

Our children deserve to grow up free from fear and to have the support of the entire community. Mother to mother, family to family, block to block, we can change the story of our streets.

Please visit our website at www.mothersforjusticeandequality.org to learn more about our work in ending violence.

Reflections to My Sisters

Mothers for Justice and Equality with Senator Elizabeth Warren

Reflections to My Sisters

About the Author

Monalisa Smith is the Founder and President of Mothers for Justice and Equality, a non-profit grassroots organization in Dorchester that aims to eliminate youth violence in Boston neighborhoods by bringing together families and communities through education and engagement. Monalisa founded MJE in 2010 following the loss of her nephew to local violence and through a "call to action," gathered fellow mothers, many of whom were also suffering the loss of a child to violence, to share their concern with the gross amount of violence against children occurring within their neighborhoods. It was then that the group agreed upon its mission to end neighborhood violence and began to believe that mothers can become catalysts for change in their communities.

Since its founding, Mothers for Justice and Equality has humanized homicide statistics through the sharing of personal stories in various media forms throughout Boston, established Monthly Empowerment Meetings and has engaged hundreds of local people in marches and rallies in support of the cause. MJE has also partnered with the City of Boston Public Health Commission in creating their first Mothers Watch Circle , which advises the Defending Childhood Initiative, and has impressed upon Governor Deval Patrick the urgency to addressing neighborhood violence. Accomplishments such as these have then allowed for MJE to receive the following awards: the Boston Business Journal's Extraordinary Leadership Award, Codman Square Neighborhood Development Corporation's Community Leadership Award, the Asian American Civic Association's Community Leadership Award, the Boston Globe 100 innovation award and recognized in Boston Magazine as an idealist influence change in Boston.

Monalisa is a Dorchester native who has used her corporate background as Director of Community Investment for Citizens Bank, Massachusetts, to help drive this movement of mothers looking to put an end to youth violence within their neighborhoods. She is a mother of 3 children and a wife. Monalisa is also a local civic leader.

Reflections to My Sisters

"MOTHER TO MOTHER, FAMILY TO FAMILY, BLOCK TO BLOCK,
WE CAN CHANGE THE STORY OF OUR STREETS."

MOTHERS

FOR JUSTICE & EQUALITY

Made in the USA
Middletown, DE
12 September 2024

60784375R00031

"MOTHER TO MOTHER, FAMILY TO FAMILY, BLOCK TO BLOCK,
WE CAN CHANGE THE STORY OF OUR STREETS."

MOTHERS

FOR JUSTICE & EQUALITY

ISBN 9781505588156

90000

9 781505 588156